MOVING AVERAGES 101

INCREDIBLE SIGNS THAT WILL MAKE YOU MONEY IN THE STOCK MARKET

STEVE BURNS
HOLLY BURNS

NEW
TRADER
U

DISCLAIMER

This book is meant to be informational and should not be used as trading advice. All traders should gather information from multiple sources, and create their own trading systems. The authors make no guarantees related to the claims contained herein. Always consult a professional before investing your money. Please trade responsibly.

FOREWARD

When did I start trading?

Looking back at my life, I don't remember a time when I was not interested in the markets. As a teen, I was fascinated by compound return tables, and the magic of growing capital over time. Before the Internet, I remember looking at stock quotes in the newspaper, and my love for trading and the markets has only continued to grow.

I have spent the last 20+ years investing and trading. My drive to be a successful trader lead to reading hundreds of trading books and putting what I learned into action. Because the learning curve was so steep, I decided to create a shortcut for new traders; the kind of information I wish I could have studied when I was getting started.

The NewTraderUniversity.com platform is that shortcut. I have condensed all the key principles that a new trader needs to know into easily understandable formats, either book or eCourse form, depending on your learning style. My goal is to get a new trader up to speed quickly, and trading successfully with very little risk.

I hope you will join me as I show you how to build and grow your own capital, with low stress and minimal risk. It will most likely be one of the most rewarding things you ever do. It was for me.

Steve Burns
@sjosephburns
Holly Burns
@hollyannburns

WHAT SOME OF OUR STUDENTS SAY

I thought about having a well-known, professional trader write the introduction for this companion guide, but I realized that this book is about you, the students that are devoting your time and energy to becoming better traders. I think it is more meaningful if you hear from our successful students:

"I have spent over a year now in intense study of the market, charting, stock trending, options, technical and fundamental trading. Learned from books, various mentor-ship DVDs, webinars, and Internet videos. I was just going from one various trade to the next, most of the time losing more than I made. I have watched your e-course several times over the past few days. Since then, I have developed a rock-solid trading plan. Anything I was having a problem with, I developed a set of rules to counteract it. Thank you so much for devoting your time to help new traders stay afloat in a sea that's filled with sharks! God Bless!"
  –Jeremy C. Rhodes

"Steve has really outdone himself on this one, the value to cost is enor-

mous. While putting most of the focus on risk management, Steve also offers plenty of information concerning technical analysis. Steve has an incredible gift when it comes to explaining difficult to grasp concepts, and he frequently shares real trades while explaining the "why" behind the trade. It is enlightening in that you can learn from the questions of others, it is not unlike the learning platform of real colleges that offer online classes. I plan on renewing membership for many years to come."

–Jim Stewart

"After going through the e-course, I have gained more confidence to build my trading plan and actually trade the plan. I got instant feed-back from you as I was trading live! Now that's something. Thanks a lot!"

–Afif

"All your guidance has helped immensely. What I've learned has given me a foundation which will never leave me as long as I trade. The risk management portion of the trading system alone has already paid dividends. Any questions I have, you've been more than helpful answering or pointing out an article you've already written. Under-standing the 'why's' of my trades has given me that 'care free state of mind'. Feels amazing. Thank you."

–Fred Robles

1

WHAT IS A MOVING AVERAGE?

I always check my charts and the moving averages prior to taking a position. Is the price above or below the moving average? That works better than any tool I have. I try not to go against the moving averages; it is self-destructive." –Marty Schwartz

I n this lesson we will learn:

- What is a moving average?
- What types of moving averages are there?
- How are they used as technical indicators?
- What time frames can they be used on?
- Which ones have I found to be the most valuable?

A moving average will be the average price for a trading instrument over a set time frame. They help smooth out the price action, and focus on where the current price is trending in relation to an average price, over the trader's time frame.

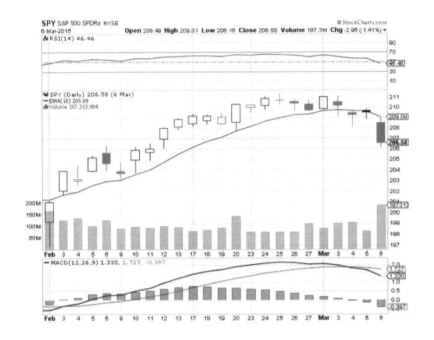

Chart Courtesy of StockCharts.com

Moving averages are technical tools used on charts for trend identification. They can be used as standalone lines for trend trading, or in conjunction with other technical indicators like the MACD, RSI, price levels of support and resistance, or even with other moving averages. Moving averages are one of the building blocks for other technical indicators like Bollinger Bands, MACD, and the McClennan Oscillator.

A simple moving average (SMA) is an indicator that shows a line on a chart based on the calculation of the average price of a trading instrument over a set number of time periods. A 5-day simple moving average is the average price over a 5-day period. If something ended the last five days at $100, $101, $99, $98, and $102, the five-day moving average would be $100.

$100+$101+$99+$98+$102= $500/5= $100

This shows the average value was $100 over the 5-day period. A simple moving average gives equal weight and importance to all prices in the time period.

An exponential moving average (EMA) gives greater weight to recent prices, to make it more reactive and faster to adjust to price action. An EMA changes faster to account for recent price action, and gives traders faster entry and exit signals than a simple moving average.

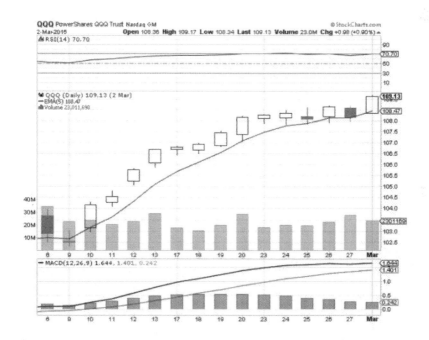

Chart Courtesy of StockCharts.com

A Weighted Moving Average (WMA) assigns a weighting factor to each price in the price period for calculation, according to its age. The most recent data gets the most weight, and each price value gets less weight as the data is calculated backwards for the prices in the time period. A weighted moving average gives more value to the most recent prices, and less as prices become older.

―――――――――

Don't get caught up in the differences or importance of these types of moving averages. In the long run, it will be the principles of your trading and the quality of your trading signals that create profitability, more than which type of moving average is the 'best'. The point is to identify and capture trends with the moving averages you choose, for your own time frame.

Moving averages are powerful tools to use in your trading. Moving averages are a great place to look for clues to what levels are key areas for support and resistance, and for trend identification. They have meaning because they are used as technical indicators as key levels to trade from, and in systematic trading for entry and exit signals. Moving averages are an unbiased trend indicator. Trend lines are subjective, moving averages are quantifiable facts.

Moving averages can be used on all time frames, intraday, daily, weekly, and monthly. Traders that trade intraday can watch moving averages on the daily chart to see how price reacts to certain levels.

The 5-day EMA on the daily chart may find support intraday, for instance. Traders can also look for a confluence of time frames, where key supports are reached on a daily and weekly time frame simultaneously, for higher probability entries due to signals on multiple time frames.

In this book, I will be focusing on how I trade using the simple and exponential moving averages on the daily chart, but their principles are the same for all time frames. Remember, the shorter the time frame, the more prices are subject to noise and the random nature of buyers and sellers. The higher you go on the time frame, the more you can see trends and the patterns of accumulation and distribution of a market, near key moving averages.

Moving averages are the simplest of all trend following indicators. In uptrends, price tends to stay above a key moving average. In downtrends, price typically stays below the key moving average. The first possibility of a change in trend is when price crosses through the moving average that it had previously been trending consistently on the other side of. Downtrends start to reverse when prices cross back up and through a moving average, while uptrends show signs of reversal when price falls through a moving average to below it.

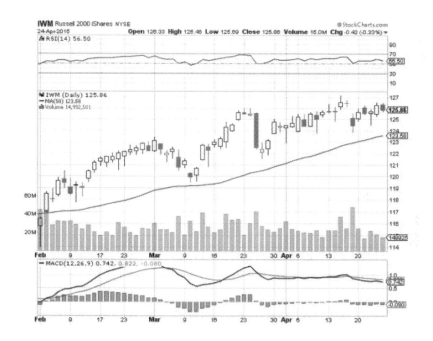

Chart Courtesy of StockCharts.com

Here is my moving average answer key. This is what each moving average means to me in my trading and how I use them:

• 5-DAY EMA: THIS IS A SIGN OF STRONG MOMENTUM. IT tracks the trend in the short-term time frame. This is support in the strongest up trends. This line can only be used in low volatility trends with strong momentum. A break back above this line is a sign for me that an uptrend may be resuming. I primarily use it as an end of day trailing stop. It is rare that this line does not break intraday, even in the strongest trending markets.

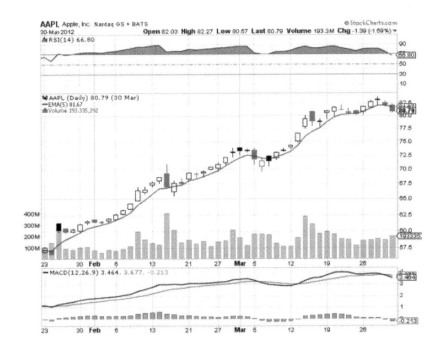

Chart Courtesy of StockCharts.com

• 10-day EMA: The 10-day EMA is a great moving average to use to keep you on the right side of the major market trend. It is usually the first line to be lost before any real trouble begins. It can be used as a standalone signal in some stocks and markets that tend to trend strongly in one direction for long periods.

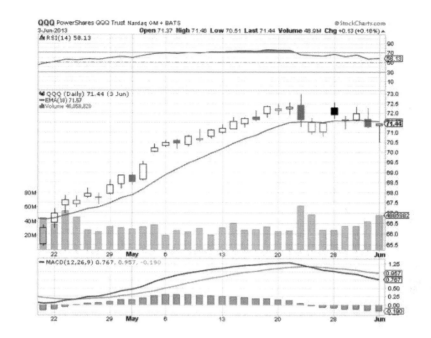

• 21-day EMA: This is the intermediate term moving average. It is generally the last line of support in a volatile uptrend. To me, it is the inevitable reversion to the mean in a market when it finally pulls back after an extended trend.

Chart Courtesy of StockCharts.com

• 50-day SMA: This is the line that strong leading stocks typically pull back to. This is usually the support level for strong uptrends. It is normal for uptrending markets to pull back to this line and find support. Most bull markets and uptrends will pull back to this level. It is generally a great "Buy the dip" level.

Chart Courtesy of StockCharts.com

• 100-day SMA: This is the line that provides the support between the 50-day and the 200-day. If it does not hold as support, there is a high probability that the 200-day SMA is the next stop. This is the deeper pullback level in bull markets and uptrends. It usually presents a great risk/reward ratio in bull markets.

Chart Courtesy of StockCharts.com

• 200-day SMA: Bulls like to buy dips when markets are trading above the 200-day moving average, while bears sell rallies short below it. Bears usually win below this line, as the 200-day becomes longer term resistance, and bulls buy pullbacks to the 200-day if the price stays above it. This line is one of the biggest signals in the market telling you which side to be on. Bull above, Bear below. Bad things happen to stocks and markets when this line is lost.

Chart Courtesy of StockCharts.com

REMEMBER:

- Moving averages are not the Holy Grail of trading. They are tools to help a trader capture a trend in their own time frame.
- Moving averages work best in low volatility markets. The more volatile the market the less respect moving averages will be given as emotions take over market participants.
- Moving averages have meaning because they are used by so many market participants.
- Moving averages are the average of past price data, they aren't predictors. Instead, they are a way of looking at the current trend.

- Moving averages are reactive technical analysis tools.

WHAT WE LEARNED:

- A moving average is an average of prices over a certain time period.
- There are simple, exponential, and weighted moving averages.
- Moving averages filter and smooth price data, and help identify trends.
- Moving averages can be used on all time frames, intraday, daily, weekly, and monthly.
- I use moving averages on the daily chart: the 5-day EMA, 10 day EMA, the 21-day EMA, the 50-day SMA, 100-day SMA, and the 200-day SMA.

2

HOW TO USE MOVING AVERAGES

"I have one strong rule and that is when it comes to a stock if it's above the 200-day moving average, I'm gonna be long it, and if it's below it, I'm either not gonna own it or I'm gonna be short it, period end of story and I just let that govern every single thing that I do." –Paul Tudor Jones

---

I n this lesson we will learn:

- Trading with moving averages instead of fundamentals
- Using moving averages as a reactive technical analysis tool
- Entering trades using moving averages
- Exiting trades using moving averages
- Capturing trends with moving averages

WHILE FUNDAMENTAL ANALYSIS IS THE STUDY OF A MARKET'S potential value, technical analysis is the study of the behaviors of the participants trading in that market. Investors are primarily focused on valuation metrics for an asset, while traders primarily trade price action.

Most investors focus on price to earnings ratios, sales growth, earnings growth, and supply and demand when trying to value markets. Technical traders look at price action on charts to see what price levels the other market participants are buying and selling. Moving averages is a price filter for traders to get a wider view of trends than just price alone.

Your goal as a trader is to develop ways to capture trends inside your time frame, through quantified methods based on proven principles and back tested market studies. Moving averages are one of the best tools for quantifying this. The incorporation of moving averages as trading signals removes much of the emotions and opinions that tend to get traders into trouble.

Moving averages are great guides for entries, exits, position sizing, and providing a filter to view the actions of buyers and sellers in a market.

Price is the result of an agreement between the buyer and the seller at any given moment. Your purpose is to be on the right side of key moving averages as a market or asset is being accumulated or distributed, inside your trading time frame.

Profitable trading is the result of making better decisions than the majority of traders that are on the wrong side of a key moving average in your market.

SOME QUANTIFIABLE SIGNALS FOR ENTERING TRADES:

- Intraday momentum buy signals as price breaks above key moving averages on daily charts

- End of day momentum buy signals as price breaks and closes above key moving averages on daily charts
- Next day momentum buy signals as price breaks and closes above key moving averages on daily charts from the previous close
- Buying support as price pulls back and holds above a key moving average
- Buying as price reverses and breaks back above a key moving average after being on the other side of it in a downtrend
- Buying a pull back to a supporting moving average in a trend
- Selling short into a moving average acting as resistance in a downtrend
- Buying when a shorter term moving average crosses over a longer term moving average
- Selling short when a longer term moving average crosses under a shorter term moving average

Possible ways to place stop losses after entry:

- A key moving average does not hold as support for a long position
- A key moving average that has acted as resistance is broken through on a short position
- It gives a trader better odds to stay in a good trade if you set your stop a few percent below a key moving average to avoid the obvious levels being hit
- An end of day stop, if price closes on the wrong side of your key moving average
- A next day stop, you close a position on the next open if your key moving average is violated
- A moving average crossover

Potential ways to set a trailing stop:

- If you enter a trade based on a longer term moving average like the 100-day or the 200-day, and it has gone into an extended profit, you can move your stop up to the 5-day or 10-day moving average
- Set a trailing stop at a loss of the previous day's low or high of day

Exit with Profits:

- Price crosses back under your initial moving average after holding it through a profitable trend
- The RSI can be used to exit a trade for maximum profit after entering based on a moving average
- Exiting your position when it becomes overbought or oversold
- Exit if the Bollinger Band is broken
- Exit if your profit target is reached

REMEMBER:

Momentum entry signals are based on the beginning of a strong move through, and break out of, a short-term trading range. Momentum trades are based on the principle of even higher highs or lower lows on a chart, based on a new trading range and trend. Momentum is usually a short-term trade. Momentum traders are looking to capitalize on a move and then get out into the follow through strength. This is where the 5-day EMA and 10-day EMA are used.

A trend trade is where you enter with the flow of the markets trend of higher highs and higher lows, or lower highs and lower lows, in your own time frame. Trends can also be measured by moving averages that are going higher or lower on the chart. This is where you use the 50-day and 100-day moving averages to capture a longer-term trend of weeks and months.

A trend following trade attempts to capture an entire trend, and will give back paper profits in search for these longer term trends. Trend followers can capture trends that go on for years. Trend followers also tend to get out of markets as trends begin to shift, and can make money taking short positions in down trending markets. Most them take their cue from the 200-day moving average.

Moving averages are not very useful tools for swing trading tightly range bound markets. They are primarily for trading trends or deep swings inside of long term trends. Some traders look for signs that a moving average in their time frame is beginning to slope upwards or downwards, and consider it one indicator of a trend beginning, continuing, or changing.

There are no magic moving averages that always lead to profitability, there are only those that allow you to make money during trends based on your own personality, risk tolerance, and time frame.

Each trader must decide how to incorporate moving averages into their own system and time frame. Moving averages are best used for trend identification and trailing stops after entries are taken based on other technical parameters. While single moving averages are not standalone signals for creating trading systems, they are one of many tools that a trader can use for signals inside their trading plan. It is possible to use moving averages as standalone signals to trade individual stocks and commodities that are under heavy accumulation or distribution, if you keep your losses small and let your winners run.

High volatility is the biggest enemy of trading with short term moving averages on a daily chart, because they are not respected during price range expansion and can cause multiple losing trades before catching a winning trade. Using moving averages of longer time frames like the 50-day, 100-day, and 200-day is a way to filter out much of the noise on the intraday and daily charts, but the trader will have to accept larger drawdowns in account capital during the volatile price moves, even in stronger long-term trends.

Moving averages can be the most valuable tool in your trading toolbox if you use them to quantify your entries and exits inside of a robust trading system. Moving averages are one of the easiest and fastest ways to quantify the trend in specific time frames.

In this book we will explore how I use them in my own trading strategy.

WHAT WE LEARNED:

- Moving averages can show traders and investors the buying and selling behaviors of market participants
- Moving averages can be used to identify a trend by what side of it prices are trending on
- Moving averages can be used to quantify current trade decisions based on the trend of previous price action
- Moving average breakouts can be used as momentum buy and sell signals
- Key moving average support levels can be used as dip buying opportunities
- Moving averages can be used in quantifying hard stops, stop losses, and trailing stops
- Moving averages can be part of a trading plan and trading system after a markets key moving averages are understood

3

5-DAY EMA (MOMENTUM)

"Moving Averages are my gurus." –Larry Tentarelli

I n this lesson we will learn:

- What is the best use for the 5-day EMA?
- What kind of market does it work best in?
- When does it not work?
- What are the dangers?
- What are some trade examples?

The 5-day EMA is best used as one tool of many for a discretionary rule based trader. The 5-day EMA does not back test well as a standalone indicator, but can be very useful in conjunction with other technical indicators for entries, exits, and end of day trailing stops.

The 5-day EMA can be used as:

- A short-term momentum long indicator to capture a few days of a trend, if price breaks above it.
- If price suddenly breaks above it after being below it for weeks.
- It can be a short position indicator if it is lost after price has traded above it for weeks.
- It can be used in conjunction with the RSI for entries and exits.
- Avoiding long entries in overbought markets or short positions in oversold markets. Trading vehicles will vary, so you must study charts in your markets to see what RSI levels are historically useful.
- It will show you the short-term trend by what side price is on, bullish above and bearish below, on the daily time frame.
- It can be used as an end of day trailing stop after entering on the signal of a longer term moving average. Enter using the 200-day SMA, and if the trade trends in your favor, exit and lock in profits after the 5-day EMA is lost and not recovered by the end of the day.
- It can be a trailing stop as you let profits run late in a trend that was entered based on a different type of entry signal.

For example:

You can enter after a break above the 200-day SMA with an end of day stop on a close below the 200-day. Then, if prices break above the 50-day SMA, move your stop to a close below the 50-day. Then to the 10-day EMA, and finally to a close below the 5-day EMA.

You can lock in profits and not have the drawdown of holding a trade all the way back to the 200-day SMA, but exiting and locking in profits.

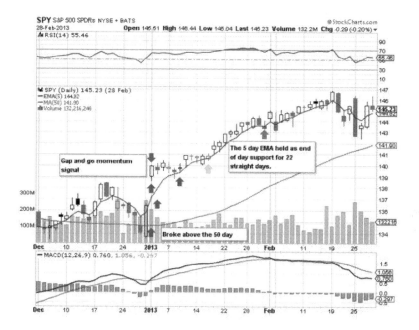

Chart Courtesy of StockCharts.com

The 5-day EMA is a great way to use a trailing stop for a winning trade on breakouts over the 50-day SMA or the 200-day SMA. This works in strongly trending markets that breakout after a long price consolidation period, and trend over a key long term moving average.

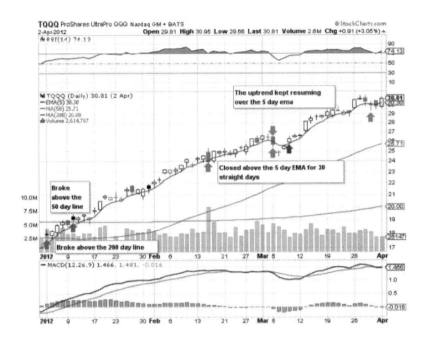

Chart Courtesy of StockCharts.com

After a downtrend into oversold territory, a strong reversal back over the 5-day EMA can be a momentum long reversal signal as it closes back over a key long term moving average.

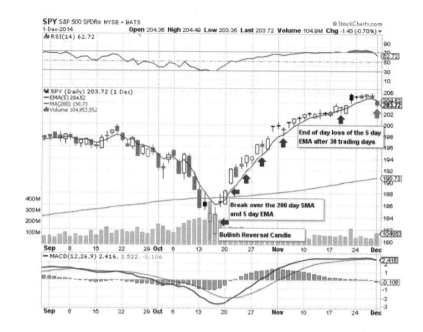

Chart Courtesy of StockCharts.com

In downtrends, the 5-day EMA can act as end of day resistance. The 5-day EMA is a great way to trail a stop on a winning trade after taking a short position on a stock that loses its key 200-day moving average, and starts a downtrend on heavy distribution.

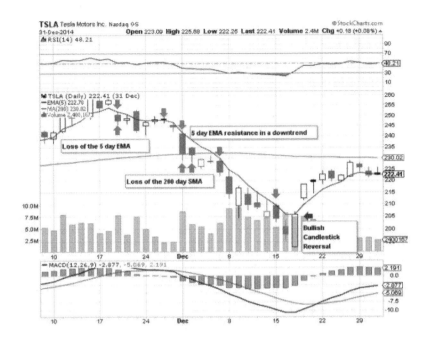

Chart Courtesy of StockCharts.com

The 5-day EMA is not helpful in markets that are stuck in a trading range, are not trending, or penetrate the 5-day EMA each day. Expansion of trading ranges are due to uncertainty in direction, and do not respect the 5-day EMA as price discovery is underway.

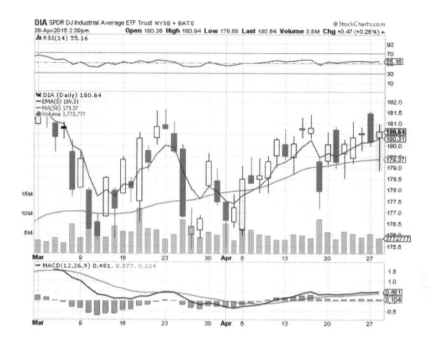

Chart Courtesy of StockCharts.com

You want to use the 5-day EMA:

- After a momentum signal like a breakout above a key trading range, very bullish candlestick, a gap and go, or a break and close above a key long term moving average like the 50-day or 200-day.
- The 5-day EMA is a great short term moving average to use in the moving average crossover systems that we will discuss in this course.
- You want to use the 5-day EMA on charts where price is staying on one side of the 5-day EMA line over multiple days and weeks. This shows that it is being respected, and price staying on one side of it for long periods of time shows strong accumulation or distribution in a market.

Be aware that the best time frame to trade with the 5-day EMA is only for 5 to 10-days in most instances. It is important to take profits as price gets extended too far above the 5-day EMA, because it typically returns to that line, and trends that strong don't last more than a few weeks to a month. The best exits are using oscillators that show overbought or oversold conditions or Bollinger Bands. We will discuss this in detail later in this book.

WHAT WE LEARNED:

- The 5-day EMA is best used as a strong momentum indicator, a trailing stop after a long trend off a longer term moving average, and an end of day stop while trend trading
- While using end of day stops, it is crucial that you position size small enough that you will not lose more than 1% of your total trading capital if the 5-day EMA is lost and volatility expands suddenly
- Be ready to step in with an emergency stop if volatility expands enough to cause you to be down 1% of your trading capital intraday
- The 5-day EMA works best in strong trends with momentum, and can be used is uptrends and downtrends
- The 5-day EMA is not useful in range bound markets or when prices are highly volatile
- The 5-day EMA can't be used as a standalone indicator due to it being a tool in strongly trending markets only. Trading with the 5-day EMA in isolation will lead to over trading and strings of losses when markets don't trend in one direction or become volatile. You should limit the amount of trades you have in a month to control how many losses you can experience, and only take the setups with the most upside potential

4

10-DAY EMA (SHORT-TERM TRENDS)

"The 10-day exponential moving average (EMA) is my favorite indicator to determine the major trend. I call this "red light, green light" because it is imperative in trading to remain on the correct side of a moving average to give yourself the best probability of success. When you are trading above the 10-day, you have the green light, the market is in positive mode and you should be thinking buy. Conversely, trading below the average is a red light. The market is in a negative mode and you should be thinking sell." –Marty Schwartz

I n this lesson we will learn:

- Using the 10-day EMA as a reactive technical tool
- It's trend capturing effectiveness
- How to filter its use
- How it keeps you on the right side of the market
- Weaknesses

The 10-day EMA is a fast-moving average and keeps a trader on the right side of a fast moving average. This line is not usable in markets that have big daily ranges that take prices through the 10 EMA repeatedly on the daily chart.

Using the 10-day EMA:

- It can be used to trade off of intraday, as the line is returned to during both downtrends and uptrends. Day traders can go long as price returns to it from above or go short as price returns to it from below
- Profitability from this moving average is by riding trends over multiple days for large wins, and taking small losses quickly when the line is breached
- It is crucial to avoid trading off the line when the market is not respecting it over multiple days
- Buying a momentum breakout over it increases the odds of a trend
- Trend trading it on the daily chart with end of day stops if the line is breached can keep you from being prematurely stopped out of a trend until it closes under it
- The higher volatility becomes the more the 10-day EMA is not useful
- The 10-day EMA can be used as a long signal only if the long term trend is up as measured by the 200-day SMA, or as a short signal only in downtrends where price is trading below the 200-day SMA

The 10-day EMA can keep you trading on the right side of market's short term trends and price swings for several straight days. The probability of catching a trend increases when a combination of moving averages are broken, like the 10-day EMA and the 50-day SMA, or the 10-day EMA and 200-day SMA.

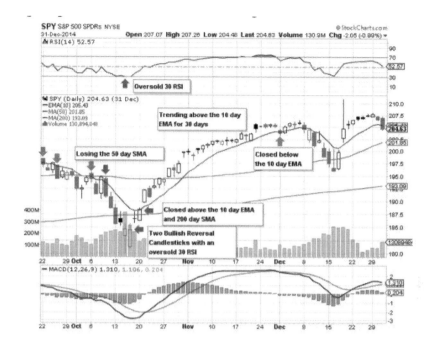

Chart Courtesy of StockCharts.com

You can see how the 10-day EMA could kept traders on the right side of the market for multiple days in the row. When using the 10day EMA, it is good to lock in profits using oscillators when price gets far extended beyond the 10-day EMA. The 30 RSI is a great place to lock in short trades, and the 70 RSI is a great place to lock in long trades.

For example, Apple breaking over the 50-day SMA and 10-day EMA then reversing back under both initially. The next trading day a 'gap and go' took Apple back over both key moving averages and started a 21-day trend over the 10-day EMA.

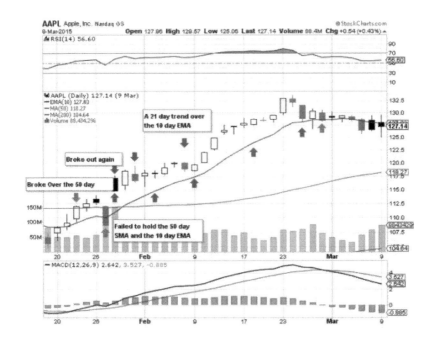

Chart Courtesy of StockCharts.com

Most good trends start with some type of momentum, a gap in prices, a break over a longer term moving average, or a large candlestick at the beginning of a trend.

There is generally a momentum ignition signal before a long run in a stock or market that has enough strength to stay on one side of a short term moving average.

It's important to stay on the right side of an uptrend with the 10-day EMA. Staying long above the 10-day EMA and exiting long positions as the RSI becomes overbought near the 70 RSI. This line will get traders out of a position before a market makes its inevitable trips back to the 50-day, 100-day, or 200-day SMA.

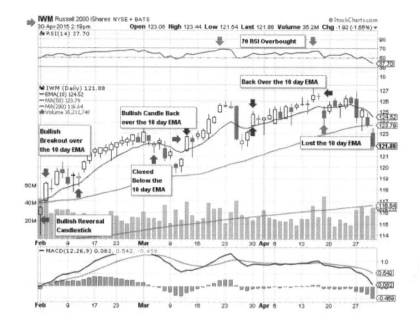

Chart Courtesy of StockCharts.com

You can choose how fast you want to lock in profits. You can enter on a break above the 10-day EMA, but you want to exit to maximize profits and not ride a winning trade all the way back to under the 10 day EMA. The end of a short-term momentum trend is usually a quick and ugly reversal. The 70 RSI is a great place to exit to maximize profits with stock indexes and big cap stocks.

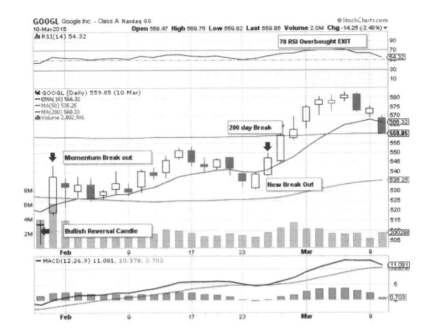

Chart Courtesy of StockCharts.com

What we learned:

- The 10-day EMA will show you the short-term trend on a chart, and it is a better guide than opinions
- The 10-day EMA can keep you on the right side of a market trend for days, weeks, and months at a time
- The 10-day EMA is a powerful trend capturing tool and improved dramatically when combined with other technical indicators for entries and exits
- Staying long above the 10-day EMA and short below it can keep a trader out of a lot of trouble
- The 10-day EMA is not effective in volatile and range bound markets.

- The 10-day EMA can't be used if it is inside the intraday price movements for days in a row. You are looking of momentum in price movement that closes on one side or the other of the 10-day EMA for multiple days
- Momentum breakouts over key long term moving averages is a great place to start a position with the 10-day EMA as a trend filter

5

21 DAY EMA (PULLBACK SUPPORT)

"Where you want to be is always in control, never wishing, always trading, and always first and foremost protecting your ass. That's why most people lose money as individual investors or traders because they're not focusing on losing money. They need to focus on the money that they have at risk and how much capital is at risk in any single investment they have. If everyone spent 90 percent of their time on that, not 90 percent of the time on pie-in-the-sky ideas on how much money they're going to make. Then they will be incredibly successful investors." –Paul Tudor Jones

I n this lesson we will learn:

- How to use the 21-day EMA as a reactive technical tool
- Trend capturing effectiveness
- How to filter its use

- How it keeps you on the right side of the market's trend
- Weaknesses

The 21-day EMA marks the intermediate term trend in a market. It gives trades more room to move and "breathe" without being stopped out for a loss prematurely due to short term intra-day price gyrations. In this example, you can see a 29-day trend in $TSLA after a break out over the 50-day. Buying the break over the 50-day with an end of day stop of a close under the 21-day EMA, would have caught about a $45 move on $TSLA.

Chart Courtesy of StockCharts.com

The Shake Shack IPO trend could have been captured by simply using a 21-day EMA as an end of day trailing stop. The 21-day EMA can keep you on the right side of a volatile monster stock in both uptrends and downtrends.

Chart Courtesy of StockCharts.com

The $TSLA chart shows it closing below the 21-day EMA for 16 straight days. This is evidence that it is being distributed not accumulated, no opinions or predictions required. A trader that shorted on a loss of the 21-day EMA could have covered their short after the bullish reversal candle, or their price target had been met.

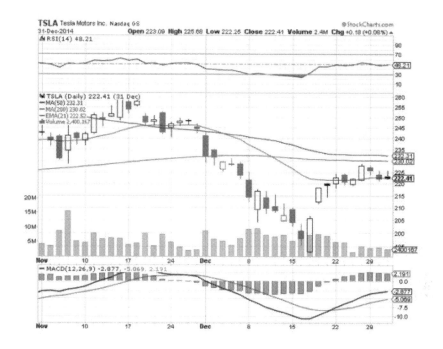

Chart Courtesy of StockCharts.com

While trading with the 21-day EMA it is important to use an exit strategy that maximizes profits instead of waiting for a return to the 21-day EMA. The RSI is one tool I use for exiting trades in stock indexes and big cap growth stocks. When price approaches the 30 RSI, I look to cover shorts, and when price approaches the 70 RSI, I look to sell my long positions regardless of what moving average I am utilizing. This is because at these extreme readings, the risk/reward has skewed against the current position, and the odds of losing profits are greater than the potential for the trend continuing.

Chart Courtesy of StockCharts.com

The 21-day EMA is a great trend trading tool that can keep you from getting stopped out of a trending market or stock, and maximize the gain from the trend by filtering out most of the intraday noise.

The 21-day EMA can be used an overlying filter for a shorter term trading system. For day traders, and those using the shorter term moving averages, they can look to take long trades when price is above the 21-day EMA, and short trades below it. Shorting resistance and buying support intraday, and using short term moving averages, have better odds of working when it is done in the direction of the intermediate trend.

Chart Courtesy of StockCharts.com

WHAT WE LEARNED:

- The 21-day EMA is a reactive technical tool that can be used to define the intermediate trend
- The 21-day EMA can be used to capture trends by trading price based on which side of the moving average price is trending on
- The 21-day EMA can be used as an entry signal for trades, and can be combined with oscillators to signal exits that maximize gains
- Prices closing consistently under the 21-day EMA defines an intermediate down trend
- Prices closing consistently above the 21-day EMA defines an intermediate uptrend

- The 21-day EMA does not work as a standalone indicator in volatile or range bound market, but needs to be combined with other indicators for long term trading success

6

50-DAY SMA (UPTREND DEFENSE LINE)

"For a market leader, the 50-day moving average - which computes a running average of price closes over the past 50 trading sessions - can act as a support level during an uptrend. But it can also act as a resistance level during a downtrend. If a stock breaks below the 50- day line in heavy volume and can't rally back, it's often a signal that buying demand is drying up and the stock's run is ending." –Ken Shreve

In this lesson we will learn:

- What time frame is it usually used for?
- What are the key uses for the 50-day SMA?
- When is it usually support?
- When is it usually resistance?
- What are its weaknesses?

The 50-day SMA can keep you in a growth stock under money manager accumulation for months. It takes times for institutions to build large positions in stocks, so their buying drives up prices. Their buying shows up as strong trends on charts, far above the 50-day SMA for months at a time.

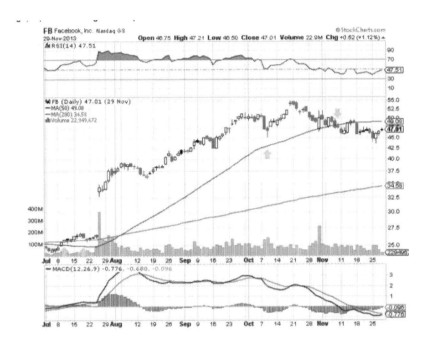

Chart Courtesy of StockCharts.com

The 50-day SMA can also be used as a filter for trading momentum strategies using other moving averages and technical indicators. A possible trading rule could be to go long on a stock when the price broke over the 10-day EMA, and was also trading over the 50-day SMA. With this filter, you would not go long on a stock over the 10-day EMA unless it was also over the 50-day SMA.

Chart Courtesy of StockCharts.com

A stock trading under the 50-day SMA is likely under distribution, and the odds are better for a long trade if it is over both the 10-day EMA with short term accumulation, and the 50-day SMA showing longer term accumulation. A strong monster stock will find buyers at the 50-day while it is being accumulated in a bull market.

Chart Courtesy of StockCharts.com

REMEMBER:

- In the strongest of Monster stocks, the 50-day can act as a standalone Green light/Red Light indicator. Staying long as price is above the 50-day line and exiting if price drops below and capture longer term trends in the process.

Chart Courtesy of StockCharts.com

- In a strong bull market trend, the 50-day SMA will hold as support many times before ultimately failing.

Chart Courtesy of StockCharts.com

- In strong trends, the 70 RSI can be broken and the market can keep rising for months at a time. The 50-day is the key line to watch as a strong bull market pulls back and has dips in price. Markets generally bounce on the first pullback to this line. However, the more a support levels is tested, the greater the odds are that it can be broken and a deeper pullback or correction occur.

Chart Courtesy of StockCharts.com

- As long as markets are trading above the 50-day SMA, the trader should be thinking "buy the dip", because selling a strong market trading above the 50-day SMA is not where the easy money is. The easiest profits are in following the trend on the long side.
- At the start of a downtrend, you will often see price break through the 50-day SMA, then become resistance. Rallies try to make it back to the 50-day SMA, but fall short, and a downtrend begins.

Chart Courtesy of StockCharts.com

- In a stock or market under distribution, the 50-day SMA can act as resistance for months at a time, and even become a short signal until the line is broken and price can stay above it for a sustained time. For a market trending lower and lower below the 50-day SMA, the direction of least resistance is to sell the market short.

Chart Courtesy of StockCharts.com

What we learned:

- The 50-day SMA can keep you in winning trades for months in the right trend
- The 50-day SMA provides support for Monster stocks under accumulation and for stock index support in bull market pullbacks
- The 50-day SMA provides support in long term up trends
- The 50-day is usually the pullback to resistance line at the beginning of downtrends in markets that are under distribution
- In strong trends price tends to get extended and run away from the 50-day leaving it too far away to use

- It is better to use other technical indicators to exit (like the RSI) and maximize profits and not wait for a retrace to the 50-day line

7

100-DAY SMA (OVERSOLD)

"Trade what's happening, not what you think is gonna happen." –Doug Gregory

I n this lesson we will learn:

- The 100-day SMA can be a key support line between the 50-day SMA and the 200-day SMA
- The 100-day SMA is a key area for dip buyers to watch for potential entries during bull markets
- The 100-day SMA offers a great risk/reward set up for long entries when it aligns with oversold conditions
- If price closes below the 100-day SMA for multiple days there is a high probability that the 200-day will be reached
- Markets often retrace to the 100-day SMA many times a year

When the 50-day support is lost in the market the next place that a trader can turn their attention to is the 100-day line for support. The odds of this level holding improves if it lines up with other oversold indicators.

In the $SPY chart, each dip to the 100-day SMA presented a good risk/reward entry as the long-term index was in an uptrend. When the 100-day SMA coincided with the 30 RSI, the odds were greatly increased for a winning trade.

The key with using moving averages is to look at them as levels of support and resistance to trade around. As the 50 day is lost I turn my attention to the 100-day SMA possible support level for a swing trade to the long side. I will stop out of a long position with a close under the 100-day SMA and will re-enter the trade on a close back above the 100-day SMA. I wait for the end of day results to see how the market reacts around the 100-day SMA to avoid much of the intraday noise.

Price can move around a key moving average many times before trending. I will step in and take a long trade if the rare 30 RSI level is reached, but that is a different entry signal than the 100-day SMA. Moving averages are significant to me based on how price closes around them. If the 100-day SMA is lost, I turn my attention to the 200-day SMA as the next level of potential support.

Chart Courtesy of StockCharts.com

In this example of the daily $SPY chart, the 100-day SMA, Oversold RSI 30-35, and the MACD bullish crossover all lined up for a triple convergence, creating great risk/reward swing long trades inside a long term uptrend. The 100-day SMA alone is one tool for dip buying, but you should also consider if other technical tools are confirming it as the potential dip buying area, or based on the chart pattern, it could go lower.

Chart Courtesy of StockCharts.com

When a stock is in an uptrend with consistently higher highs and higher lows, the 100-day can provide a great risk/reward re-entry if price bounces near the 100-day SMA. A bounce can happen as price approaches the 100-day SMA, but never reaches it. Look for a long bullish candlestick, an upward moving average, bullish MACD crossover, and oversold conditions to buy when the price doesn't makes it to the 100-day SMA.

The key to using moving averages like the $FB chart, is for your winning trades to be large and your losing trades to be small. You must use trailing stops to maximize your great entries like the first signal on the chart, and cut your losers quickly if you entered on the second 100-day SMA bounce.

You must also move on to other opportunities if a key moving average has lost its value as support, and not incur multiple losses as volatility increases around what was once a key support level. Limiting your entries to only those based on multiple technical confirmations will help increase your winning percentage, and limit your losses.

The 100-day SMA can be the last support before a market comes out of a range and trends strongly from over an oversold low RSI of 30-35, to being oversold above the 70 RSI in one, long trend. Your ability to capture and ride these trends will be a large part of your success as a trader.

Chart Courtesy of StockCharts.com

In the $USO chart example, a 100-day SMA breakout while the MACD was still bullish, and one that broke above the 100-day SMA with a bullish MACD crossover. Commodities and growth stocks tend to have the trend power to break over the 70 RSI and keep going, while stock indexes and sector ETFs tend to find strong resistance at the 70 RSI if it trends that far. A break and close above the 70 RSI is a momentum trend indicator, and it signals that price has gone parabolic. This can happen with commodities and the trend continue.

Chart Courtesy of StockCharts.com

WHAT WE LEARNED:

- If the 50-day SMA is lost, the next level to look for a bounce is the 100-day SMA during bull market uptrends
- The 100-day SMA is a price level to watch for a potential dip buy in an uptrending market
- If the 100-day SMA coincides with the oversold levels of 30- 35 RSI, it presents a good risk/reward ratio entry in most markets
- The price stays under the 100-day SMA for a number of

days, the greater the chance it will trend down to the
200-day SMA

- The more days in a row that the 100-day SMA breaks
through the 100-day SMA, the less meaning and
usefulness it has in a chart
- There is a good chance that the market that you are
trading will retrace to the 100-day SMA several times a
year, even in bull markets. This is normal and no reason
to panic or believe the uptrend is over.

8

200-DAY SMA (THE BULL'S LAST STAND)

"My metric for everything I look at is the 200-day moving average of closing prices. I've seen too many things go to zero, stocks and commodities. The whole trick in investing is: "How do I keep from losing everything?" If you use the 200-day moving average rule, then you get out. You play defense, and you get out." –Paul Tudor Jones

I n this lesson we will learn:

- The 200-day SMA is the long-term trend filter for a market
- The 200-day acts as the last level of key support in bull markets
- Many traders use the 200-day SMA as a trend following filter for their entries and exits
- The 200-day is one of the most watched moving averages in the market

- Long trades have a better probability of success above the 200-day SMA, and short trades have better odds below it

Staying on the right side of the long term up trend can be as simple and staying long above the 200-day SMA, and going to a cash position below it. If you take nothing else from this book, understand that **a loss of the 200-day is your first warning of a possible correction, down trend, or bear market**. This fact alone can save you from large losses.

Chart Courtesy of StockCharts.com

When investors and traders are trapped in cash after a long bear market and don't know when to get back into stocks, an entry on the first break, and close above the 200, presents the trader with a good risk/reward entry at the beginning of the next possible bull market.

Of course, they must be ready to exit if price begins to close below the 200-day SMA and the momentum fails to turn into a trend. Leading growth stocks first key support is the 50-day SMA, but their last key support is the 200-day.

Chart Courtesy of StockCharts.com

A bounce at the 200-day SMA for a monster stock presents an outstanding risk/reward ratio for a growth stock that is normally under accumulation, but during a market correction pulls all the way back to the 200-day SMA, due to equities as an asset class being under distribution. This is a technical trader's safety margin for owning a growth stock at a great entry price.

Chart Courtesy of StockCharts.com

The 200-day SMA can provide strong support in range bound markets for growth stocks that will explode into an uptrend during bull markets.

Chart Courtesy of StockCharts.com

The first sign of an individual stocks being under distribution is the loss of the 200-day SMA. After this line is lost a strong down trend can proceed quickly.

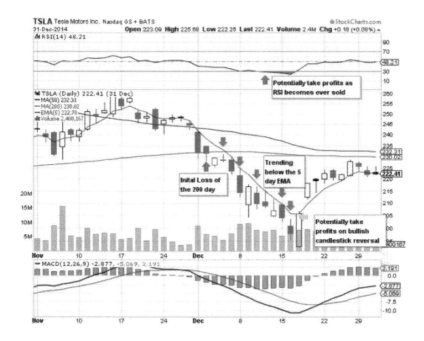

Chart Courtesy of StockCharts.com

When a stock breaks down under the 200-day SMA, it tends to rally back to the 200-day at least one more time before starting a strong downtrend. After using the 200-day SMA loss as a short entry signal, the 5-day EMA or 10-day EMA can be used as a trailing stop depending on the historical volatility of the stock. Use the key moving average that works on the stock in the past that remains unbroken for weeks at a time.

Chart Courtesy of StockCharts.com

The 200-day SMA gives the trader the ability to quantify the market environment they are in, as well as the long-term trend of that market. It shows the long-term distribution or accumulation of an asset class or market. The 200-day SMA is the ultimate line in the sand that divides bull markets from bear markets. Bulls start giving up and selling their holdings below this line, while bears begin to short rallies back up to this line. Strong moves can occur as this line is reached and then broken in one direction or the other. Battles can go on for days at the 200-day SMA, as a new trend tries to establish itself, or an old trend must be overcome. This line is a much better way to quantify the market trend, as opposed to opinions, speculations, and predictions.

Strong bull markets that have momentum and make new all-time highs must first overtake the 200-day SMA. By being long as the 200-

day SMA is broken to the upside, it gives the trader or investor a chance to be on the right side of a bull market.

Markets that have long term downtrends must first cross the 200-day SMA before any damage can be done. By exiting long positions when this line is lost, traders and investors have a chance to preserve capital from the risks of larger market corrections or bear markets.

Staying out of large drawdowns in capital can improve long term trading and investing results. Taking short positions as the 200-day lost gives traders exposure to profit from market downtrends.

Taking a short position as the 200-day is first lost has a good risk/reward ratio for the short side if a downtrend begins. A stop loss can be set at a close back over the 200-day SMA.

What technical signal should have saved investors from the 2008-2009 relentless downtrend? Understanding that the long term uptrend had changed once the 200-day SMA was lost. Long term trend followers should not be long markets under the 200-day SMA, and swing traders should not be buying long positions under the 30 RSI.

Chart Courtesy of StockCharts.com

WHAT WE LEARNED:

- The beginning of up trends and bull markets generally start as price breaks and stays above the 200-day SMA
- The first sign of the beginning of a downtrend or bear market is when price breaks and stays below the 200-day SMA
- The 200-day is the default moving average setting on most charting software. It is used by many traders to buy a break above this line, and sell short a break below it. Some buy on the break, others wait for confirmation on the next day's open or close
- As the 200-day SMA line signals whether the market is

in a long term uptrend or long term down trend, buying weakness on pullbacks above it and selling short strength below it puts swing traders on the right side of the market's accumulation of distribution

- Bad things happen to long positions under the 200-day SMA

9

MOVING AVERAGE CROSSOVER SYSTEMS

"Most of this trend following "science" can be explained by a decent moving average crossover. Don't over-indulge in complexity." –Jerry Parker

I n this lesson we will learn:

- Moving average crossover systems are a way to capture trends by entering a trade when a shorter term moving average crosses over a longer term one, then exiting as it crosses back under
- Moving average crossover systems are a way to trade based on price trends instead of personal opinions or fundamentals
- A moving average crossover system can keep you in a trade longer than a moving average alone
- A moving average crossover system will give less signals than a moving average alone

- Moving average crossover systems can be back tested for results in different types of market environments using web based tools

One way to use moving averages in a trading system is by using two moving averages that give buy and sell signals when a shorter term moving average crosses over a longer one. Legendary trend trading pioneer, Richard Donchian, used a five and twenty day moving average crossover system for buy and sell signals. Donchian was a pioneer in trading based on technical price action as opposed to fundamentals, opinions, and predictions.

The systematic way to use multiple moving averages as trading signals and smooth out entries and exits during volatile periods, is to develop trading systems using moving average crossovers. Using two moving averages, you can create entry signals that are triggered when the shorter term moving average crosses over the longer term moving average. The exit or reversal signal is triggered when the shorter term moving average crosses back underneath the longer term moving average.

Your trading time frame and back tests determine which moving average best suits your trading vehicle, time frame, and methodology. Short term moving averages can generate false signals before catching a trend, and generate more signals than systems with longer term moving averages. A trader can test the performance of different lengths of moving averages that fit their own time frame and holding time preferences.

Longer term moving average crossover systems can give back profits before the exit is triggered. The underlying principle is that you develop a moving average crossover system that enables you to have big wins and small losses. The purpose of moving average cross-over systems is to replace opinions and predictions with a quantifiable way to capture trends.

A moving average crossover system waits for a double confirmation of a trend, and forces the trader to act based on what is happening in the market due to the price trend, and not their own personal beliefs. This alone is a huge edge over the majority of traders that are simply trading from their gut. The best predictor of a future trend is the present trend that is going in the direction of least resistance until it stops.

Moving average crossover systems should decrease the amount of trades and losses as opposed to using a moving average system alone. With single moving averages, price may penetrate and go through a key moving average 3 to 5 times before trending in one direction, causing multiple losses. A crossover system may only have one entry and one exit in the same time frame. By using moving average crossover systems as opposed to single moving averages, the quality of your signals increase and the noise of false signals decrease.

OPTIONS FOR CROSSOVER TRADING SYSTEMS:

• Traders can have filters, so they only trade the long side of crossover signals when the shorter term moving average crosses over the longer term, if their market is trading over the 200-day SMA, for example. It's a good idea in the stock market because it tends to have a bullish bias thanks to the constant demand for stocks, as they are ownership in companies.

• Traders can trade the short side only if the shorter term moving average crosses under the longer term moving average, if the market is trading under the 200-day SMA, for example.

• Traders can use an 'always in approach', staying long as the short term moving average crosses over the longer term moving average. They can then exit their long and sell short, as the shorter term moving averages crosses under the longer term moving average. This approach works best with commodities, as they tend to trend in both directions, based on the current supply and demand.

• A trader can also have a 'stay in cash' signal based on high volatility, average daily range expansion, or after a series of losses. A trader could wait for a more robust signal before reentering the cross-over system.

• A trader can also add the RSI as an additional trend filter, taking only dip buying or momentum signals if they line up with their RSI parameters, or only going short at overbought levels. Mine are the 30-35 RSI as an oversold buying opportunity for most stock vehicles, 50-60 momentum long signal during uptrends, and 65-70 as the overbought level to look to exit longs or take short positions.

• The MACD crossover can also be used as a secondary filter, taking only signals when MACD is also confirming in the direction of the crossover trend signal.

• For a purely mechanical system, you must trade the technical signals exactly how you back tested them for the opportunity to get those same results, and not disrupt the system.

• Unlike single moving averages that rarely work as standalone technical indicators over multiple market environments, moving average crossover systems can be standalone trading systems that can outperform market returns and beat buy and hold investing over the long term.

POPULAR MOVING AVERAGE CROSSOVERS. CHOOSE THOSE THAT are right for your time frame and market:

5-day SMA / 20-day SMA
5-day EMA / 50-day SMA
10-day EMA / 20-day EMA
10-day EMA / 50-day EMA
15-day EMA/ 30-day EMA
15-day EMA / 150-day EMA
10-day SMA / 200-day SMA
50-day SMA / 200-day SMA

Here is one simple system that can be used to increase returns and decrease drawdowns in markets with wide price swings:

The 10-day EMA / 30-day EMA crossover signal in both directions. You go long when the 10-day EMA crosses over the 30-day, and exit the long and go short when the 10-day goes back under the 30-day. This enables the trader to capture the up swings and the down swings in a market with wide moves in both directions.

Chart Courtesy of StockCharts.com

The key to using any trading system like this will be that your winning trades will be big and your losing trades will be small. You can catch both uptrends and downtrends for profits in a two-sided market, and stay on one side of a trending chart for long periods to maximize gains in both directions.

It is crucial in studying charts and back testing for moving average crossover systems that you test and view data through multiple market environments. A long only system that works great in bull markets may be unprofitable in bear markets, or may take you to cash at the beginning of a downtrend with no trading signals for months. While the short side of the crossover may result in multiple losses during bull market uptrends, it could result in a huge win in a market plunge.

Realize that the big wins are the hardest to take in real time when rallies move against your position and cause a drawdown in paper profits. You must commit to following either a mechanical or discretionary trading system, and stick to your plan no matter what.

Be flexible with your opinions about where the market price will go, but be disciplined with your system and trading rules. It is crucial to trade a position size that allows you to trade a system without being shaken out of a trade because you can't handle the heat of a market's move against you.

In the $QQQ chart, it shows that 10-day EMA/ 30-day EMA crossover system alone would have taken a long only strategy to cash before the 2008 market meltdown avoiding the entire meltdown and an always in system that would have reversed and gone short would have captured a huge trend. In a trend of this magnitude, the RSI was not helpful as an oversold indicator, but the MACD did give some short long side swings that could have netted small gains.

Strong sustained parabolic trends like this one are where moving average crossover systems are the most profitable. However, these are rare and generally only happen every decade or so. But your moving crossover system will generally keep you on the right side of a big trend when it occurs.

Chart Courtesy of StockCharts.com

One thing that trips of system traders is that they abandon good trading systems during bad market environments. Don't abandon good long-term trading systems based on bad short-term results.

Moving average crossover systems that rely on trends to be profitable will have multiple losses in tightly range bound or volatile markets. The key is to keep them small, and take the next entry for the chance to capture the next big winner. Keep drawdowns small by trading a position size that keeps each individual loss to 1% of your total trading capital. You can trade larger position sizes with stock index ETFs, but must trade smaller with more volatile growth stocks.

Option trades could be positioned as 1% of your total trading capital, so there's no need for a stop loss. It will be an all or nothing trade where the nothing gained would be a 1% loss.

This $QQQ chart would have become frustrating in real time, as 2015 became a tightly range bound market, and paper profits would vanish as no trend emerged week after week. The good thing about this 10-day/30-day EMA cross as a standalone system, is while it kept giving back paper profits, it limited the quantity of losing trades. It saved commission costs and kept a good winning percentage through many choppy reversals, day after day.

This is the great thing about making trading decisions primarily at the end of the day, you avoid the vast amount of intraday noise.

Chart Courtesy of StockCharts.com

Long term trend followers have a signal known as the 'Golden Cross' which is when the 50-day SMA crosses up through the 200-day SMA. This is one signal that catches the beginning of long term equity bull markets.

Chart Courtesy of StockCharts.com

The $PCLN chart shows combining moving average crossovers with discretionary rule based trading using technical indicators. With this example, you would enter short trades as the 10-day EMA crossed under the 50-day EMA, and cover your short trade as price became oversold at 30 RSI. You would enter long as the 10-day EMA crossed back over the 50-day EMA and exit as the RSI went over 70 into overbought conditions.

The second signal was before earnings, so it was a riskier trade that could only be taken if your rules allowed for the risk of trading through earnings. This is how to incorporate moving average crossover signals into a discretionary rule based signals, and maximize profits without having to wait for the next crossover to exit with profits.

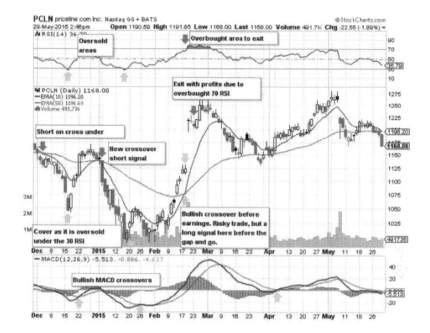

Chart Courtesy of StockCharts.com

Remember:

- Long only moving average crossover systems can greatly limit drawdowns in capital during bear markets. Many longer term systems can decrease drawdowns by 50% or more by avoiding long exposure when the market is in a downtrend.
- Moving average crossover systems that reverse and go short can be profitable in bear markets, but under perform in bull markets when downtrends don't occur, and the short side is repeatedly stopped out.
- Moving average crossover systems are trend following systems that will be profitable dependent on the market's

trend and the trader's ability to follow their system with discipline and not abandon it during losing streaks. I highly advise a mechanical back test of any moving average trading system before live trading as a base for your system's winning potential. Then you can adjust in discretionary rules to maximize winning trades and minimize losing trades.

- Moving average crossover systems can be profitable, but can also produce an uncomfortable equity curve in real time trading, depending on the trader's time frame and the market volatility. You can smooth out profits and losses with a volatility filter and go to cash when VIX becomes too high for your specific time frame.

WHAT WE LEARNED:

- To use a moving crossover system, enter when a short term moving average crosses over a longer term one and then exit when it crosses back over from the other direction
- Moving average crossover systems are usually used as a mechanical trading method for trading a market through price action alone. Discretionary rules can be added but they are generally mechanical to ensure consistent performance. When used as a purely mechanical system it can remove the stress and emotions of a trader needing to make decisions
- Using a moving average crossover system instead of moving averages alone lowers the quantity of your trades, so it both increases your chance of capturing a longer trend, and it lowers your commission costs and churn rate of trades

- Purely mechanical moving average crossover systems can be back tested for historical performance
- Moving average cross over systems can filter out a lot of the noise in a chart and give signals with better odds of a true trend emerging than with moving averages alone.

10

COMBINING MOVING AVERAGES WITH OTHER INDICATORS

"Oscillators are calculated using a derivative of price and thus most oscillators will appear very similar in shape. Stochastics, RSI, moving average oscillators and MACD are some of the more widely used oscillators. They are most useful in active swinging markets and will have less value in a flat, sideways market." –Linda Raschke

I n this lesson we will learn:

- Entering with a key moving average break as an entry, and exiting to maximize profits
- How to lock in open profits without having to wait for price to retrace all the way back to the key moving average
- How to use the RSI in alignment with moving averages
- How to use MACD in alignment with moving averages
- Technical filters to use along with moving averages

Single moving average systems don't typically back test well as standalone systems for entries and exits. They are just one tool for trend capturing, and need another layer of signals to decrease the noise and keep a trader on the right side of a market trend.

The **RSI** is a technical momentum oscillator that compares the amount of recent gains to recent losses to try to read the overbought and oversold levels of a market's price action. The RSI has a range of 0 to 100. A market is supposed to be overbought with a reading of 70. For traders this is an indication that it may be time to sell their long positions at this high reading. The RSI reaching 30 is supposed to signal that an asset is starting to be oversold and may present a good risk/reward ratio to go long at that level. Center line crosses at the 50 can be used as the beginning of a trend in the direction of the break (+51 bullish or -50 bearish).

Or the traditional use of the RSI for swing trading is best used in stock indexes and sectors with the 65-70 range indicating overbought and look to exit longs there and the 30-35 range indicating oversold and a buy signal. The RSI oscillator works best for swing trading in range bound markets. It does not work for indicating extremes in trending markets, as higher highs or lower lows happen for extended period of times. In this example of the $INDU chart during a swing trading market, it shows how the RSI signaled overbought and oversold levels. The best entry on the chart was when the 30 RSI converged with the 200 day and a MACD bullish crossover for a very high probability long trade.

RSI is not a standalone indicator, but should be used in conjunction with other trading tools for confirmation. I advise traders to stop out of long trades when the RSI closes below the 30 RSI and stop out of short trades if price closes above the 70 RSI. When price breaks out and closes beyond these levels, it is a sign of a potential parabolic move which is more common in growth stocks or commodities, but can happen in any market. The key to using the RSI is to maximize winning trades and minimize losing trades.

Chart Courtesy of StockCharts.com

The MACD is technical indicator that attempts to measure momentum of a market's price action. It converts two moving averages into two lines on a chart by subtracting the longer term moving average from the shorter term moving average being used in its calculations. The MACD shows the relationship between two moving averages of prices.

The formula the MACD uses to calculate its lines comes from the 26-day exponential moving average and the 12-day exponential moving average of a market. The 26-day EMA is subtracted from the 12-day EMA to create a line. Then the nine-day EMA of the MACD itself is also placed with the sum of the first lines to create signals for entries and exits based on crossovers. The second line is used as a signal line as it crosses over the first.

MACD is about the relationship between two intermediate term moving averages. Its signals are based off convergences and divergences of these moving averages. The convergence of the two lines indicate the likelihood that a market is in a trading range. A divergence of the two lines as they move away from each other occurs during trends in that market. The MACD is primarily used for trend and swing trading signals on crossovers of the MACD line over the signal line.

The MACD is not useful for identifying overbought and oversold markets. Instead, it is a measurement of convergence and divergence of two moving averages around a 'o' line. The MACD is good at showing potential entries based on changing momentum and can give a general bullish or bearish signal for a market trend. While the MACD can be used as a crossover system, it is best used as a tool alongside other indicators. The MACD works best in trending and widely swinging markets, and is not helpful in tightly range bound markets as it tends to go flat as price moves sideways for long periods of time.

To sum up the MACD:

When the black MACD line is over the red signal line, it is an indication of upside momentum and an uptrend, when the red signal line falls below the black MACD line, it is a signal of downside momentum and a potential downtrend. The best risk/reward entry is typically when the lines cross, because it is a signal that a potential trend or swing in price has begun.

Chart Courtesy of StockCharts.com

The $INDU chart shows how the 10 EMA/ 50 EMA cross can be used to trade price action. With the first entry, the crossover in December, the strong trend continued for seven months with small retracements before continuing higher. In a strongly trending market, a crossover system alone will work well.

Chart Courtesy of StockCharts.com

This is trend following in its most simple form. In the powerful trend, the 70 RSI and the MACD bearish crossovers lead to small pullbacks inside a powerful long term trend. This example shows a powerful trend, and then a swing trading market, and how the RSI and MACD can be used as signals to exit trades initiated by the moving average crossovers.

After June, the RSI and MACD signals began to work again as the market started to trade inside a wide range. The stock market tends to trend upwards over long periods of time. At the beginning of that chart, the MACD and RSI signals would have caused the trader to minimize the gain, and then after June, their signals would have allowed the trader to maximize the gain. This demonstrates the catch 22 of adjusting with more signals than moving averages alone.

Notice that the traders would have still done well in both market environments. However, swing trading signals will cause traders to underperform in strong trends and outperform the market in range bound markets. We must choose to trade to maximize a trend and be willing to risk open profits, or be willing to lock in profits and give up potentially greater gains, to limit risk exposure and limit drawdowns in trading capital.

When trading in the stock market with moving averages, understand that your long side trades risk/reward ratios diminish as your position gets closer to the 70 RSI, and your short position risk/reward ratio diminishes as you get closer to the 30 RSI, and the potential for an oversold bounce.

When you are long the market and the MACD is on the bullish crossover side, your odds are better for an uptrend. If you are short and the MACD is on the bearish side of the crossover, your odds for a successful short trade is greater.

Moving averages and MACD crossovers tend to be the best plan for entering at the beginning of a potential trend, while the RSI is best for showing you were to exit at the end of a trend or swing in the market price.

In system creation, chart studies, and back testing you can create filters for your moving averages.

EXAMPLES:

- You take your crossover system long trades only when the MACD is on the right side of a bullish crossover
- You only take long crossovers when RSI is above 50 for momentum signals, and take sell short signals when RSI is under 50 showing a loss of momentum
- You do not take breakouts over key moving averages when RSI is over 65 due to the skewed risk/return ratio
- You could turn off your short sell signals when the market you are trading is over the 200-day SMA
- You could turn off your long signals when the market you are trading is under the 200-day SMA

In bull markets, the 50 RSI support may be a confirming signal to enter long positions on dips, while bear market rallies to the 50 RSI may be confirmation signals for short trades.

This example of the $SPY chart from the bull market of 1999-2000 shows that even in bull markets, it is difficult for the big cap stock indexes and big cap stocks to close above the 70 RSI or below the 30 RSI.

Chart Courtesy of StockCharts.com

The key is knowing that you have these levels to work with as resistance and support when you decide to exit your profitable long and short positions. These levels work in most markets, as prices tend to get extended and then revert to the mean. They are a great way to measure your remaining reward versus your existing risk.

In a strongly trending market, or when price swings in a wide range, the MACD line crossovers will put the trader on the right side of the market in most instances, and will keep the trader on the right side of the current price trend or swing if the price continues to move in their favor.

HERE ARE POTENTIAL ENTRY AND EXIT STRATEGIES TO consider:

- Enter on a break and close above the 200-day SMA, stop loss is a close back under the 200-day. If it trends the trailing stop could be a close back under the 10-day EMA with a target of the 65 RSI on the daily chart
- Enter a stock as it bounces off the 50-day SMA. Stop loss is a close back under the 50-day SMA. Trailing stop in a trend is a close under the 10-day EMA. Target is the 70 RSI
- Enter when a stock index is at a 34 RSI but still over the 200-day SMA. Your initial stop loss is a close below the 30 RSI
- Your trailing stop is a close below the previous day's low of day. Your target is the 50 RSI
- You take a short position in a stock index as it rallies back to the 51 RSI, but the market is under the 200-day SMA
- Your stop loss is a close over the 54 RSI. Your trailing stop is the previous day's high of day. Your target is to cover your short at the 32 RSI

Position sizes must be small enough so that if your stop loss is hit, you lose a very small percentage of your trading capital. I position size and place stops so if I am stopped out, I will only lose 1% of my total trading capital. But if my trade trends in my favor, I could return 3% or more on my total account.

The whole point of this technical entry and exit module is to minimize losses and maximize gains. Your trading profitability will be determined largely from your ability to create big wins when you are on the right side of a trade, and suffer small losses when you are wrong side of a trade.

Use the market's price action to create reactive signals based on key levels of support and resistance. Get rid of your opinions and predictions and embrace price action, it is the only thing that pays.

WHAT WE LEARNED:

- Moving averages can be used for entries and as the indication of the beginning of a trend, but exits can be maximized with oversold and overbought oscillators like the RSI
- Profits should be locked in as a trend goes far enough to skew the risk/reward ratio against the current position, making the risk no longer worth the potential remaining reward
- Traders should look to exit long positions as the RSI approaches the 70 RSI, and look to exit short positions as the RSI approaches the 30 RSI on the daily chart in most markets. This could vary in different markets so back test and chart studies are crucial
- A trader can use the MACD crossover as a filter to confirm taking a moving average break to decrease the amount of trades and increase the accuracy of entries
- A trader can use the MACD and RSI to confirm moving average entries, and as filters in system creation and back testing

Ready to take your trading to the next level?

Join thousands of other trading students at New Trader University! Our eCourses are created especially for those just starting out in the markets.

NEW- Technical Trader Video Newsletter

Sign-up for our new video newsletter service, and **every Sunday, Tuesday, and Thursday**, you'll receive videos of Steve's detailed chart analysis and back testing results for 20 of the best ETFs and stocks. Follow market trends *while* they're happening and ask Steve questions anytime.

Join the Technical Trader Video Newsletter today!

New Trader 101

The place to start for new traders! Become successful with less stress. In the New Trader 101 eCourse, you'll get:

- 13 high quality videos covering how and why to trade
- Real trade examples with detailed charts
- The most powerful trading psychology and stress management techniques being offered today.

Join New Trader 101 today!

Moving Averages 101

Everything you need to know to harness the power of Moving Averages! In the Moving Averages 101 eCourse, you'll get:

- 11 high quality videos covering how to get started with Moving Averages
- Real trade examples
- More than 45 annotated charts

Join Moving Averages 101 today!

Price Action Trading 101

Master the concepts of reactive technical analysis and learn the best times to get in and out of your trades! In the Price Action Trading 101 eCourse, you'll get:

- 17 high quality videos covering the best way to enter and exit your trades for a profit.
- Step-by-step examples
- More than 30 annotated charts

Join Price Action Trading 101 today!

Options 101

This 19-part video course is packed with information about Options, and how they can help you up your trading game. It includes real trading examples, many visuals, and an Options Play Strategy Guide that you won't find anywhere else. In the Options 101 eCourse, you'll get:

- 19 high quality videos covering how and why to trade
- Step-by-step trading examples
- Many annotated charts

Join Options 101 today!

Real Trade Examples: Volume 1

Have you ever wanted to have a private consultation with Steve? To see how and why he trades the way he does? This is your chance at a fraction of the cost of a one-on-one consultation. Steve will show you step-by-step how he enters, when he exits, and the signals that he follows for maximum profitability.

These 19 real trade examples have interactive, annotated charts and downloadable PDFs that you can use to take your own trading to the next level!

Join Real Trade Examples: Volume 1 today!

Did you enjoy this eBook?

Please consider writing a review.

Listen to many of our titles on Audio!

Read more of our bestselling titles:

New Trader Rich Trader (Revised and Updated)

Moving Averages 101
So You Want to be a Trader
New Trader 101
Moving Averages 101
Buy Signals and Sell Signals
Trading Habits
Investing Habits
Calm Trader

Made in the USA
Middletown, DE
13 October 2018